The Wesleys of Epworth

by

John Haden and KS2 Pupils from
All Saints CE Primary School,
Belton,
St Martin's CE Primary School,
Owston Ferry,
Wroot Travis CE Charity School
and Epworth Primary School.

First published by Barny Books,
All rights reserved
Copyright © John Haden 2009

No part of this publication may be reproduced or transmitted in any way or by any means, including electronic storage and retrieval, without prior permission of the publisher.

ISBN No: 978.1.906542.02.3
Publishers: Barny Books
              Hough on the Hill,
              Grantham,
              Lincolnshire
              NG32 2BB

              Tel: 01400 250246

Copies of this book may be obtained from:

Julian Bower Associates,
Julian Bower House, Louth,
Lincolnshire, LN11 9QN
Tel/Fax: +44(0)1507 601254
www.captainjohnsmith.co.uk

Contents

		Page
1.	300 years ago	5
2.	After the fire	19
3.	At Oxford	28
4.	Living at Wroot	35
5.	Going to America	43
6.	Hearts strangely warmed	50
7.	Riding through England	58
8.	Singing the gospel	64
9.	Marriages made in heaven?	67
10.	Practical help for the poor	72
11.	The world-wide parish	74
12.	The triumphs of his grace	77
	Sources and Thanks	79

The Old Rectory Physic Garden, Epworth,
North Lincolnshire

1. 300 years ago

On the night of February 9th 1709, a five year old boy was trapped in an upstairs room at the Epworth Rectory. *'I was in bed. Suddenly I woke up as there were shouts from outside saying "Fire, Fire!" I was getting hotter and hotter. As I got out of bed I realized that smoke was coming under my door. I scrambled around my room trying to reach the window. Then I saw it, my chest. I dragged it to the window and climbed onto it. Someone in the yard must have seen my face at the window as he shouted to his friend to get onto his shoulders. Then another man followed, then another and very soon they'd made a human ladder and the one on top could just reach me through the window. He brought me down. A few seconds later, the burning roof caved in.'*

(by Joseph A. and Matthew B.)

Saving John from the fire

John Wesley never forgot his escape from the fire and throughout his life showed the same single-minded determination. His mother, Susanna, was convinced that this rescue was nothing less than a miracle, part of God's plan for John's life. Steeped in the King James Bible from childhood, she began to think of John in the words of the Prophet Zechariah as a *'firebrand plucked out of the burning'*. Two years after the fire, she vowed to God *'to be more particularly careful of the soul of this child that thou hast so mercifully provided for...that I may do my best endeavour to instil into his mind the principles of thy true religion and virtue....'*

Nobody knew who started the Rectory fire that night, but the suspicion was that it was not an accident. Samuel Wesley, John's father, was not a popular Rector. The Rectory had been set on fire previously and the local people had burnt his crops, wounded his cattle and even attacked his dog. He was a stern man with a strong sense of the importance of his position.

Rev Samuel Wesley by Gavin B.

Both Samuel and Susanna came from families who were dissenters, who objected to the way the Church of England was run. Samuel's father died when he was very young so his mother sent him to Dorchester Grammar School to get a good education. He wanted to go on to Oxford University but dissenters could not go, so he changed his views and became a member of the Church. He was so poor that he had to walk to Oxford and once there, supported himself through his studies at Exeter College by working as a servant of the other students.

(by Jack B. and Daniel L.)

Susanna was the youngest of the twenty five children of the scholar and preacher, Dr Samuel Annesley. She was his favorite daughter and he ensured that she had a good education at a time when this was very unusual for a girl. Although he was a very popular preacher, he had to leave his Church living when he refused to accept the requirements of the new Prayer Book of 1662. In spite of this dissenting background, Susanna came to believe when she was thirteen that it was wrong to dissent. Like Samuel, she accepted that her loyalty should be to the Church.

They probably first met at Susanna's sister's wedding, and then exchanged letters and occasionally met when Samuel visited her father at home. Both highly intelligent and with strong characters, Susanna admired Samuel's learning and he was attracted by her beauty. Their loyalty to the Church of England had brought them together and they were married in Marylebone Parish Church on 12th November 1688. She was nineteen and he was twenty seven. Samuel had been ordained into the Church of England ministry when he completed his degree and he found a post as a curate in London. They started life together on an income of just £30 a year.

Always short of money, Samuel decided to earn more by serving as a naval chaplain on a man-of-war. But as soon as his ship came into port, he left to rejoin his young wife. Their first child, Samuel, was born the following year. They found that a curate's income was simply not enough to live on and Samuel was ambitious to have a parish of his own. In 1691, he found what he was looking for, or rather was given it, the living of a village parish in the beautiful Lincolnshire Wolds at South Orsmby just south of Louth. Their income rose to £50 a year and they settled into the parsonage. Soon more children arrived although not all of them survived.

St Leonard's Church, South Orsmby, Lincolnshire

Samuel took his parish duties very seriously and even found time to take up his writing. He had already published a collection of poems, with the strange title: *'Maggots or poems on several subjects never before handled'*. Now he could get down to more scholarly work, starting a study of the Book of Job which he wrote in Latin and which took the rest of his life to complete.

South Ormsby Hall, the home of the local squire, lies just below the church and the whole community was centred on the lives of the squire and his family. The Wesley's time at South Ormsby ended suddenly when Samuel came home one day to find an elegant lady sitting with Susanna in the kitchen. She was not the Squire's wife but his mistress. Samuel was furious that such a woman would dare to visit his wife.

Susanna Wesley from the portrait in the Old Rectory

Samuel demanded that the woman leave the house and told her not to come back. The Squire was not amused and Samuel was forced to resign from his living. They had to leave their home with their three children and find a new church and a new rectory. Fortunately, Samuel still had the support of his patron, the Marquis of Normanby. After a brief spell as curate in another parish near Louth, he was invited to become the Rector of Epworth in the far north-west of Lincolnshire.

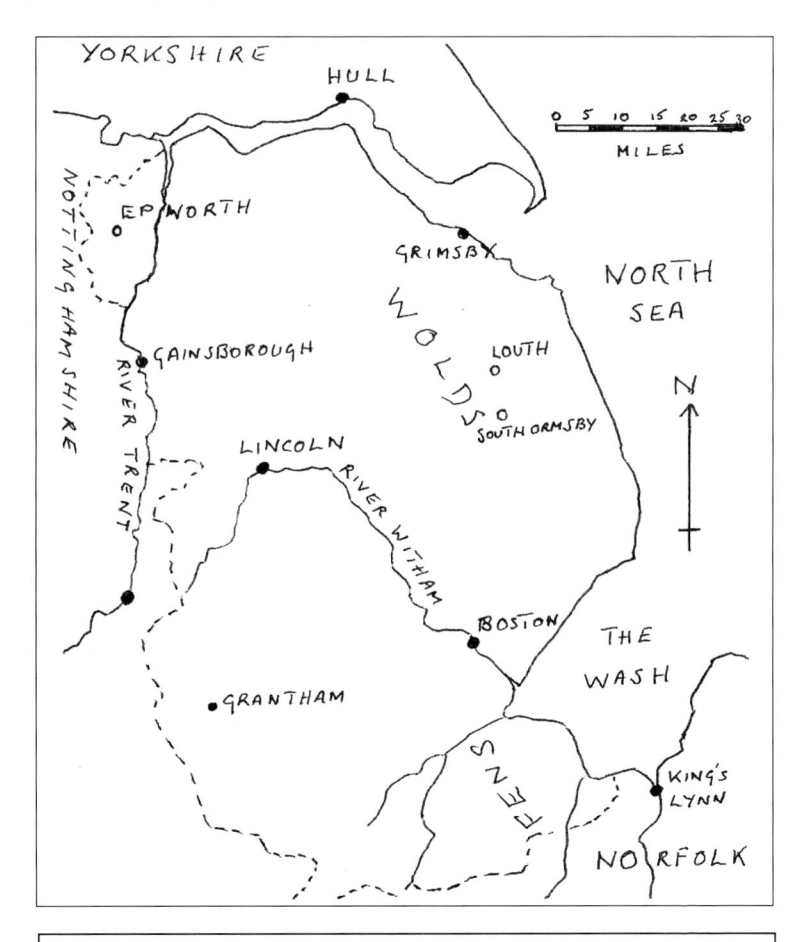

Map of the County of Lincolnshire by the Wesley Book Team

They travelled with all their belongings over the Wolds to Lincoln and then north-west to Gainsborough to cross the River Trent. It was about a hundred miles by very rough roads to Epworth and into a very different world. The town of about one thousand people was built on a slight rise above the low peat country of the Isle of Axholme, surrounded by rivers and flooded in winter.

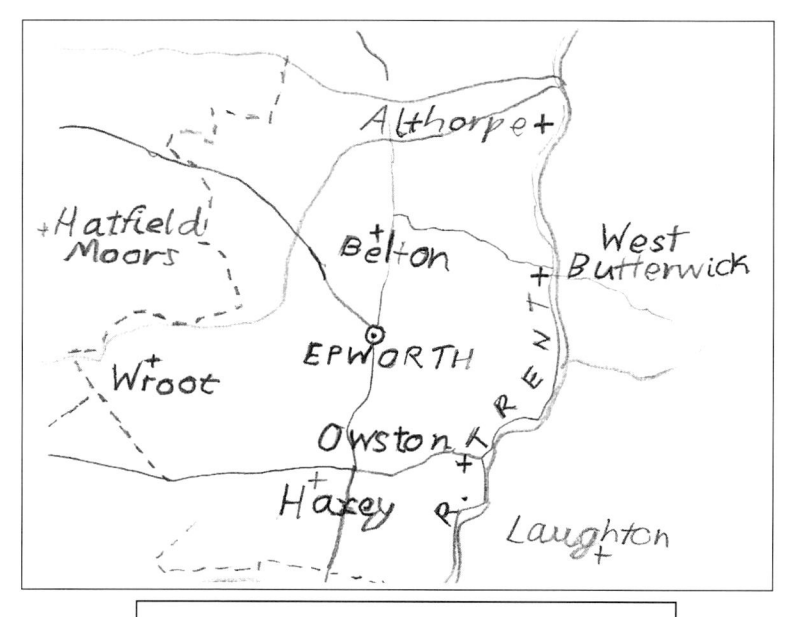

The villages of the Epworth area by Max B.

The people of the Isle, or Islonians, did not take kindly to outsiders. Not long before, a Dutch engineer called Vermuyden had agreed with King Charles I to drain the water-logged land to improve it for agriculture. In exchange, Vermuyden and his partners were given the rights to one third of the land. But this also meant that the local people lost their rights to use the marshland as they had for generations, for grazing their cattle, fishing, shooting duck and geese and for cutting peat for fuel from areas called turbaries. They objected violently to these changes and the disputes went on for years.

St Andrew's Parish Church, Epworth

The Isle was also a stronghold of religious dissent with many Baptists and Quakers holding their own church services. The Scrooby Separatists who had escaped from England to Holland and then went to America as the Pilgrim Fathers came from North Nottinghamshire not far away to the west. Epworth was not an easy place for any Rector to work and there was bound to be trouble when Samuel Wesley with his High Church views, belief in the divine right of kings and insistance on church discipline came to minister to the tough, independent and outspoken people of the town. Few were educated and many tempted to violent reaction to change.

For the Wesleys, the first challenge was to furnish the large Rectory to accommodate their growing family. Although the Epworth living brought £200 to the Rector, some of it had to be collected as tithes (one tenths) paid unwillingly by the parishioners from their farming income and some from the eighteen acres of church land around the Rectory which the Rector was expected to farm himself.

The croft at the Old Rectory where the Rector's sheep grazed.

It would have been better for Samuel to have followed Susanna's advice and hire a farmer to manage the land but Samuel was determined to farm it himself however poor the yields. Soon he was deep in debt.

Coming out of church one Sunday, Samuel was amazed to be arrested. He had borrowed £30 from a man called Pindar from Owston Ferry who wanted his money back. When Samuel could not pay, he was taken off to jail in Lincoln. Susanna Wesley tried to get her husband out of prison by sending him all her jewels including her wedding ring, but Samuel refused to take them. So he had to stay in jail. A couple of months later, Samuel's friends raised enough money to pay the debt and get him out.

(by Holly J. and Melissa B.)

The gates of Lincoln Castle by Hannah P.

With her husband in prison, Susanna was desparate for help. Samuel had written to the Archbishop of York who kindly came to visit her in Epworth. Asked if the family had enough to eat, Susanna replied, '*I will freely own to your Grace, that strictly speaking, I never did want bread. But then, I had so much care to get it, before it was ate and to pay for it after, as has often made it very unpleasant to me. And I think that to have bread on such terms is the next degree of wretchedness to having none at all.*' Archbishop Sharpe left her a sum of money to keep the family going.

Meanwhile, in the prison, Samuel found that his fellow debtors were a more fruitful field for his ministry than his truculent parishioners. He told the Archbishop that the prison was like a paradise in which he could yet do good sending for books to help him teach those who shared his fate until, after some months, he was released and went home. His friends advised him to leave such an unwelcoming place as Epworth but Samuel was resolute, writing again to the Archbishop that *'I confess I am not of that mind, because I may yet do good there; and 'tis like a coward, to desert my post because the enemy fire thick upon me'.* He returned to the Rectory and to Susanna's bed.

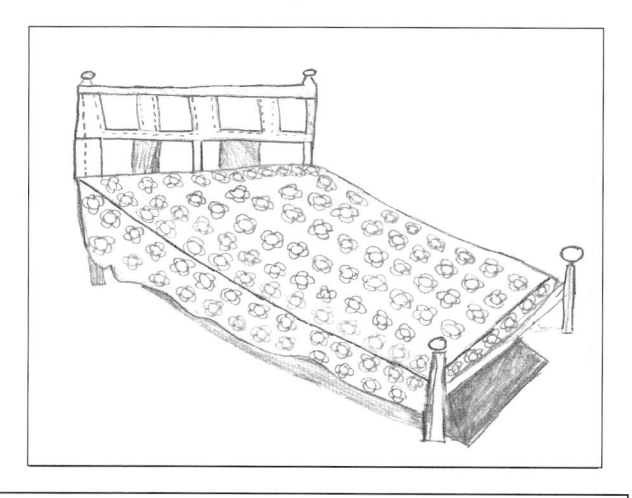

Early 18th century bed in Epworth Rectory by Joseph A.

It was the bed, or rather who was in which bed, that was at the heart of the major quarrel which the Wesleys had in 1701. Every morning, they and the children had family prayers including a prayer for the King's majesty. This was no problem for either of them while James II was on the throne, but when William of Orange became king, Susanna thought of him as a usurper. As John Wesley later reported: *'Sukey,' said my father to my mother one day after family prayers, 'why did you not say amen this morning to the prayer for the king?' 'Because,' said she, 'I do not believe the Prince of Orange to be king.' 'If that be the case,' said he, 'you and I must part; if we have two kings, we must have two beds.' My mother was inflexible. My father went immediately to his study; and after spending some time with himself, set out for London...'*

Samuel did not come home until the following year, and even then he planned to return to make arrangements for the parish and then leave his wife for good. But as he was leaving the town, he met a Minister who persuaded him that he should go home and seek Susanna's forgiveness. He turned around and returned to organise the rebuilding of their home and to share his wife's bed once more. In the following year, their second son John was born.

Epworth Old Rectory from the garden

For all his faults, Samuel worked hard as the Rector of Epworth. He provided two services every Sunday, visited his parishioners even when they did not wish to see him and dealt with any whose behaviour he judged to be sinful. Those who broke their marriage vows were made to stand on the cold church floor without shoes and naked apart from a sheet over them. A man whom he caught taking the ears off the corn which he brought as a tithe was marched to the Market Cross and publicly denounced. He baptised the children of the town's folk, following the practice of 'triple dipping' which must have put all but the most robust newborn at risk, especially in mid-winter. He even set up mid-week classes for the more committed of his congregation called the 'Epworth Society'. His may not have been a fruitful ministry but it was a devoted and determined one and he faced those who attacked his family, his crops and his home with great courage.

The silver chalice presented to Samuel Wesley by his patron the Marquis of Normanby in 1706 and used by John and Charles.

Only nine of their nineteen children survived infancy and one died in a terrible accident. *When one of Susanna's babies was born, she got a lady to look after it because she was so tired and the baby was poorly. That night the baby was in the lady's bed. Meanwhile, outside, a group from Epworth who didn't like the Wesleys, came to the Rectory and started to make a lot of noise so that nobody got much sleep. The lady who was looking after the baby fell asleep* with the baby still in the same bed. She rolled over and smothered it. The next day, she woke up with a cold baby under her. She took the body straight to Susanna and said, 'I'm sorry, I've smothered your baby.' Susanna was devastated. *(by Ciar G. and Robert H.)*

Susanna's children by Joshua M.
First came Samuel in 1690,
Shortly followed by a child who died.
Then Emilia was born but sadly after her
Two children who strangely died.
Then came Susanna, most beautiful of them all,
And Mary was born to be one of the gang,
Followed by Mehetabel, kind and helpful.
Then sadly followed by five children who died
And Anne was born, the smallest of the troop
Of children walking down the road.
Then came John, the king of them all
And shortly after, another baby died.
Then came Martha, Charles and Kezia
Three in three years, to make it nineteen.

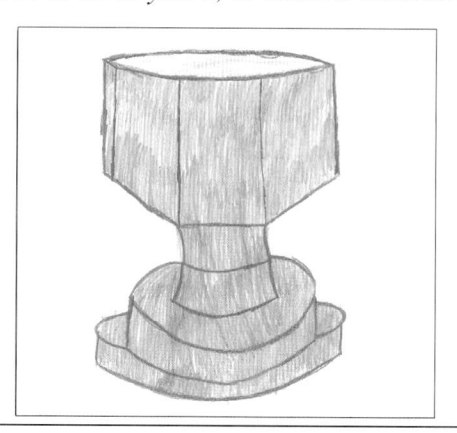

The plain medieval font in Epworth Parish Church in which Samuel Wesley baptised twelve of his children, by Brad C.

2. After the fire

As the embers of the Epworth Rectory burnt themselves out, Samuel and Susanna realised just how much they had lost. Shivering in the cold night air, they at least knew that all the children were safe. Even the youngest girl, Martha, then three, and Charles, the baby of the family, had escaped. Their eldest boy, Samuel, had already been sent to school in London and the second, John, had been rescued by neighbours from an upstairs window. Although all his books and even a manuscript he had just finished were gone, Samuel knelt in his nightshirt in the garden. *'Let us give thanks to God! He has given me my children; let the house go, I am rich enough.'*

For Susanna, heavily pregnant and badly scorched from her attempts to return to the house, the future must have seemed totally daunting. Her carefully managed home was in ruins and her family had to be boarded out with relatives and neighbours in the town picking up all sorts of undesirable habits from other children. To rebuild his house, Samuel borrowed more money. Some was raised by subscription and some from the Church Commissioners. What is now the 'Old Rectory' is actually the new one, built for about £400 and completed by the end of 1709. As the work went on, Samuel set about rebuilding his parish duties and getting his garden back into cultivation.

Two months after the fire, Susanna's nineteenth child, Keziah, was born prematurely. As soon as she could, she got her children back into their new home and and re-established their orderly domestic world. This centred around their discipline and education. In her own words, Susanna's children were taught from one year old to *'fear the rod and to cry softly'* so that the *'odious noise of the crying of children was rarely heard in the house'.* Her eldest son, Samuel, in fact did not speak at all until he was five years old. When she called to him to ask him where he was, *'Here I am, mother,'* he replied from under the kitchen table!

The kitchen at the Old Rectory

From then onwards, Susanna decided that each child should begin formal schooling on their fifth birthday. She taught them for six hours a day, six days a week. The children rose at 5 in the morning, said their prayers and had their breakfasts. Lessons began at 9 and went on until 12. At midday, the children ate at a table alongside their parents, each child eating *'what was set before it'*, without comment or complaint. If they needed anything, they were to whisper their request to the maid, *'pray give me .....'.* and they were taught to address each other as *'Brother John',* or *'Sister Kezzy'.*

In the afternoon, the little ones were rocked to sleep in their cradles for a set time, while those over five returned to their lessons, from 2 until 5. *'There was no such thing as loud talking or playing, but everyone was kept close to business for the six hours of school. It is almost incredible what a child may be taught in a quarter of a year by vigorous application, if they have but a tolerable capacity and good health',* wrote Susanna. Under this vigorous regime, she was able to teach all her children, except Kezia, to learn their alphabet in one day and to read in three months. She insisted on high standards of behaviour and set up 'Eight Rules or Bye-Laws' of the Rectory to govern their lives.

Susanna Wesley's Eight Rules or the Bye-Laws of the Epworth Rectory

1. Whoever is charged with a fault of which they are guilty, if they confess and promise to amend, shall not be beaten.
2. No sinful action, lying, pilfering, etc., shall ever pass unpunished.
3. No child shall ever by punished twice for the same fault, and if they amend, shall not be criticised for it afterwards.
4. Every act of obedience shall be commended.
5. Any child obeying or doing anything intending to please, even if not done well, shall be kindly accepted and the child encouraged to do better.
6. Property rights must be respected and none allowed to interfere with the property of another, even if it is only worth a farthing or a pin.
7. Promises are to be kept and a gift once given is the property of the one who receives it.
8. No girl shall be taught to work until she can read well; this rule is to be followed so that girls are not taught to sew before they can read as so few women can now read fit to be heard.

With so many children, Susanna needed to set aside time to talk to each of them as individuals. So she allocated to each a private session on different days of the week. *'On Monday I talk with Molly (Mary), on Tuesday with Hetty (Mehetabel), on Wednesday with Nancy (Anne), on Thursday with Jack (John), Friday with Patty (Martha), Saturday with Charles, and on Sunday with Emily (Emilia) and Sukey (Susanna) together.'* This enabled Susanna to give each of her children the spiritual guidance and nurture which would stay with them for the rest of their lives.

She also needed time for herself and set aside an hour from five each afternoon to spend in study and in prayer. While her children helped each other to read the Bible, Susanna had time for her own writing as well as helping Samuel with his great work on the Book of Job. There is even a lovely story of Susanna's way of signalling to the family that she was not to be disturbed. When their mother pulled her apron up over her head, that was it – don't bother her!

The Old Rectory from Rectory Road, Epworth

Samuel and Susanna were ambitious for their children's education and dismissive of opportunities in Epworth. They both taught them all that they could and then decided to send the boys away to the best schools they could find, while the girls stayed at home. Samuel the eldest was sent to Westminster School in 1704 although his father had to borrow money to pay the fees. Fortunately, after three years at school, Samuel won a King's Scholarship which guaranteed free education. He was the finest scholar of the family and his success at Westminster continued when he was given a post as *'Usher',* or assistant schoolmaster.

Samuel, John Wesley's older brother

When John was ten, he was nominated by his father's sponsor, the Marquis of Normanby who was a governor of Charterhouse School in London, for a free place there, becoming a *'gown boy'*. John's father advised him to *'take a morning run three times round the Green'* to make him fit for a tough life at school but it must have been hard. *He used to get bullied and had his meat taken from him. So he lived on bread and water but he survived on it. (by Jamie W.)* He later wrote *'I believe that so far from harming me – this formed the basis of lasting health.'* In spite of the hardship, John did well at Charterhouse and was well-liked by the other boys.

Charterhouse School in the early 18th century by Max B.

Two years after John left home, Charles followed him down to London and was admitted to Westminster School. His brother, Samuel, invited him to live with him and his wife, reducing the cost considerably. He also proved to be a good scholar and earned a reputation as a good fighter, defending other boys from bullies. When he was thirteen, he too won a King's Scholarship and moved into the school itself with the other boarders. With all three brothers in London, they must have met frequently, staying with Samuel at his Westminster lodgings and enjoying his wife's cooking. As Epworth was so far away, they hardly if ever went home during their school years although Susanna wrote reguarly to all three of them and Samuel would have seen them on his regular visits to London.

The Rector of Epworth had been elected as a representative for the Lincoln Diocese on Convocation, the Church's governing body. This gave him a very welcome excuse to escape from the rural backwater of Epworth and meet up in London with his clerical friends to discuss the latest theological ideas. Each time he left Susanna and the children behind, he made arrangements for his parish duties to be covered by his poorly paid curate. These regular visits were a life-line for Samuel, even if they put more strain on his finances and on his wife. Her ordered management of the Rectory provided his children with a secure home, but it also get her into difficulties with the Curate.

On Sunday evenings when her husband was away, Susanna would gather the household together in the Rectory kitchen and lead a time of prayer and worship for them all. Susanna found in Samuel's papers a collection of sermons by two young Lutheran Missionaries to South India and read these to her kitchen meetings. Soon these informal acts of worship attracted her neighbours who found her meetings much more helpful than the services led by the Epworth Curate. Attendance at Church dwindled as rapidly as the numbers grew in the Rectory kitchen.

When nearly two hundred people crammed in to hear what she said, the Curate's patience snapped. Writing to Samuel away at Convocation, Mr Inman complained that such gatherings were actually illegal as they were not services in church led by the clergy. It was most improper for them to be led by a woman who was also the Rector's wife. Samuel saw the justice of his case and wrote to Susanna instructing her to stop the meetings.

She took her time to reply, then defended what Inman had called a *'conventicle and others called a puppet-show'*. She knew that the meetings had done much to build good relationships with the parishioners and that they had been helped by the sermons she had read to them. She told Samuel that *'families which very seldom came to church now go constantly.'* She suggested that her husband should *'take some time to consider'* before agreeing with the demands of *'the malicious, senseless objections of a few scandalous persons, their laughing at us and their censuring us.'* She would obey him, but only if he sent her his *'full and positive command in such full and express terms as may absolve me from all guilt and punishment for neglecting this opportunity of doing good to souls when you and I shall appear before the great and Awful Tribunal of our Lord Jesus Christ.'* Faced with such determination, Samuel very wisely backed off and quietly left her to get on with both the meetings and her pastoral work even when he was not away from Epworth.

Not long after John Wesley went away to school, the family at the Rectory began to experience strange noises and events which they could not explain. It seemed that the place was haunted by a ghost. *The first sign of 'Old Jeffrey', as he was nick-named by Emilia, was when one of the servants heard a knock on the kitchen door followed by a groan. He opened the door to find no-one there. The door was knocked on three times further that night and feeling a little scared, the servant went to bed. He then heard what appeared to be a turkey gobbling and the sound of someone stumbling over some boots. The following day one of the maids heard a knocking on a shelf and she was so scared that she dropped the tray she was carrying and fled.*

The next evening, Mary Wesley was sitting reading in the dining room when the door opened and she heard the rustling of a silk dress. She saw no-one but was aware of a person walking around her. Getting up, she slowly walked from the room thinking that there was no point running as whatevever it was would be able to catch her anyway! She told Susanna, her sister, at supper and they heard a knocking under the table. The door latch was also going up and down. The girls told their mother, who said that she would have to wait to see for herself before she was convinced.

She didn't have to wait long. One of the girls called her to the nursery, where she heard the sound of a cradle being rocked. But there was no cradle in the room and there hadn't been one there for years. One of the girls, Hetty, actually saw a man walking down the stairs, wearing an old night-shirt, but her mother Susanna thought it looked more like a headless badger. *(by Lauren B.)*

Samuel Wesley decided to send Anne up into the attic to blow loudly on a trumpet to frighten away whatever was disturbing them. Anne was only sixteen and terrified, but she bravely went up the stairs and blew for all she was worth. The noises stopped, but then started again not long after. It seemed that the Wesley family would have to live with 'Old Jeffrey', whoever or whatever he was.

All the Wesley family took the haunting of the house by 'Old Jeffrey' seriously. John and Samuel collected all their accounts of what happened and John published them many years later. As far as he was concerned these disturbances were supernatural. He even came to believe that the ghost had been sent to punish the Rector for vowing to separate himself from Susannah. John shared the general belief of the time in the reality of '*witchcraft and apparitions*', rather than blaming the disturbances on the practical tricks of the Epworth people wanting to disturb their unpopular Rector and his family.

3. At Oxford

When Samuel left Westminster School, he continued his academic success at Christ Church, Oxford. When he had completed his Masters degree, he was elected a 'Student', as Fellows of Christ Church were known. This helped his younger brothers to follow in his footsteps and it must have given their father great satisfaction to have all three of his sons become members of the grandest of all the Oxford Colleges. *Christ Church is both a church and an Oxford University College, named in honour of Jesus Christ. John Wesley started his student days there when he was 17 and was educated at Christ Church from 1720 to 1725. While he was there he became a serious Christian, having read the book 'The Imitation of Christ'. He received a bachelor's degree in 1724.*

(by Joseph A.)

When John Wesley joined Christ Church, he was awarded an 'exhibition' of about £20 but it was not enough to live on. His brother, Samuel, helped by letting him use a college room but he had little to spare for the social activities of the other students. He also suffered from ill-health until he read a book that suggested that the secret of good health was *'temperance and exercise'*.

John began to follow a vigourous life-style, eating simply, rising early and getting as much exercise as possible by riding his horse, a regime that kept him remarkably fit for the rest of his long life. As he studied to complete his degree, John wrote home to both his father and his mother for their advice on whether he should go into the church as an ordained minister. His father counselled a delay. Although he was keen for John to follow him as a clergyman he felt that more study should come first. Susanna wanted him to be ordained as soon as possible so that he could come back to Epworth to help his father. Although he was not sure, she argued, the best way of finding out was to be ordained and then see whether this was what God was calling him to do. John as usual followed his mother's advice and was ordained Deacon by the Bishop of Oxford in Christ Church Cathedral on 27th August 1725. From that day onwards, he was a Church of England clergyman.

Earlier that year, John had met the pretty daughter of the Rector of Stanton, a village about thirty five miles north-west of Oxford in the Cotswolds. Sally Kirkham had two sisters and a friend of theirs made up a quartet of young women with whom John Wesley was soon very friendly, particularly with Sally. The long ride out to Stanton, walks in the countryside together and the pretence that they all had classical nick-names, led to John's falling in love. She was the first of a long line of women whose relationships with John were a confusing mixture of passion and religious seriousness.

When Sally married someone else, John kept writing intimate letters to her, behaviour which Susanna thought quite improper and about which even he felt some guilt. At about the same time, John started to keep a very private diary in which he recorded his own faults and failings alongside the rules which he set himself. Brought up in a household of seven sisters and a dominant mother, it is not surprising that John should find it difficult to relate to women, but he was also sure that God sent women into his life so that he should be able to lead them to faith. The problem was that they found it hard to tell whether it was the love of God or the love of John Wesley that he was offering!

One thing was clear though, he could not marry because he had no money. There was avacant fellowship at Lincoln College for which he could apply as it was limited to men from Lincolnshire. Perhaps, with Sally married to another, John sought safety in a role which could only be held by an unmarried man. He applied for the fellowship and soon his father could declare with pride, *'my Jack is a Fellow of Lincoln College'*. The fellowship provided John with lodgings and a small income, but this was not paid until the end of the year, so for a time, he had nothing to live on.

Lincoln College where John Wesley was a Fellow from 1726

John had to go home, walking all the way north to Epworth taking a month for the journey. Once home, John could help his father by taking over some of his duties as he was an ordained clergyman. John was soon enjoying the country again, riding and shooting, and visiting local families.

Kitty Hargreaves' name appeared in his private diary for 1726. She was the daughter of a local widow and John became infatuated with her. Little messages began to appear in code in the diary, *'never touch Kitty again!'* etc. John was struggling to reconcile his pastoral duties with his interest in young women. It was a friendship which lasted three years without disaster before John had to return to Oxford, summoned by the College to get on with the duties of his fellowship.

His brother Charles had followed him to Christ Church in 1726. With only three years between them, John and Charles were close as brothers, although Charles remained in John's shadow for much of his life.

Charles Wesley by Connor S.

John warned him to take his studies seriously and to avoid too much social life, to which Charles is said to have replied, *'what, would you have me to be a saint all at once?'* Although he was too poor to indulge in much partying, Charles enjoyed life as a student. When John went back to the Epworth area, Charles was no longer living in John's shadow and began to develop a more serious side, which proved difficult at Christ Church. *'A man stands a very fair chance of being laughed out of his religion…..in a place where 'tis scandalous to have any at all.'* He felt he needed the support of other students of a like mind to encourage him to practice his faith.

So it was Charles who invited a small group of friends, some at Christ Church, some from other Colleges, to form a religious society. They met in each other's rooms on different days of the week, attended Communion together and started to visit the sick and the poor. They visited debtors imprisoned in Oxford, and William Morgan, one of the group, even visited a condemned murderer held in Oxford Castle.

When John Wesley returned to Oxford in 1729, he joined Charles in these meetings, at first sharing the leadership of the society. Both had become College tutors, John at Lincoln and Charles at Christ Church. Both also encouraged the tutorial students in their care to join in their religious acitvities. As the society grew, John took over more and more of the leadership. The group attracted the ridicule of many students and came to be called 'the Holy Club', 'Bible moths' and even 'Methodists', because they were so methodical in their approach to faith.

Tom Quad, Christ Church where Charles Wesley at one time had rooms as a Fellow, or Student, of the College.

John encouraged the group to became more committed to private prayer and public worship and to pointing out each other's failures and faults. He introduced questions they had to ask themselves each day on different aspects of the Christian faith and encouraged them to follow a punishing life-style, rising each day at 4 am and fasting on two days each week.

Trying to follow John's fanatical demands led to Charles and William Morgan making themselves ill. William went home to Ireland where his family were horrified at his state. He died there three months later from what they thought was the result of 'excessive fasting and religious hysteria'. Word got back to Epworth of John's behaviour and both his father and his sister, Emily, told him to stop adopting such extreme religious enthusiam. His brother, Samuel, came to Oxford to see what he could do, advising Charles to take more care of his health. He also told John that he was needed back in Epworth to help his father, but John's response was to become increasingly detached from his family. He claimed that he had to focus on his Oxford duties where he could serve God better than he could amongst the '*lukewarm Christians*' of Epworth. He even stopped writing to his mother, although Charles continued to write.

As John's behaviour became more extreme, it was Charles with his open and friendly nature who encouraged two key young men to join the Oxford Methodists as their group became known. The first was Benjamin Ingham, a student at Queen's College who chose to meet with Charles in Christ Church but avoided John Wesley. The second was a student from Pembroke College, George Whitefield, who was so poor that he worked as a servant to other students, much as Samuel Wesley had done. Charles Wesley encouraged both Ingham and Whitefield and both became leaders in the Methodist movement, Whitefield becoming famous as a gifted open-air preacher.

George Whitefield

4. Living at Wroot

In 1724, Rev. Samuel Wesley took on the living of parish of Wroot to earn more money. In those days, clergymen could hold as many livings as they liked, retaining the income from each parish and appointing a young Curate to carry out their duties at little cost. Wroot brought in an extra £50 each year to help Samuel meet his debts, and in 1727, John Wesley agreed to help his father at both Epworth and Wroot.

Samuel, Susanna and those of their children still at home moved house to the Wroot parsonage so that their fine Epworth Rectory could be rented out. Their tenants were their daughter Susanna, or Sukey as they called her, and her husband, Richard Ellison, a wealthy land-owner from the Epworth area. He was a coarse and violent man but rich enough to support their family of four children and to occupy his father-in-law's Epworth Rectory.

If the town of Epworth was a rural backwater in Susanna's eyes, Wroot must have seemed the end of the earth. It was so inaccessible that it was even known by some people as *'Wroot out of England'! Wroot today is a little village of about a hundred houses. We have a lot of rain and a lot of wind but living here is peaceful. At harvest time there are a lot of tractors and big farm machines going everywhere and they are very, very slow. We have two churches, a pub and a shop, and many farms. Our school is very small and friendly with only twenty nine children which makes us a very, very small school!* *(by Niall C.)*

At the end of the village, opposite the church gate, there is a special post which was built at the end of 1999 to celebrate the coming of the new Millennium. Around the base of the post there is a seat, higher up a picture of John Wesley and at the top of the post a beacon basket. This was lit for the first time at midnight on New Year's Eve 1999. In the Wesley's time, a beacon would have been used to signal important news such as the British victory at Blenheim or the crowning of George II.   *(by Hannah P.)*

Coming into Wroot village from the south, past the beacon.

The Wroot Parish Church has been rebuilt since the Wesleys' time but it still stands on the same site in a graveyard at the end of the village. Sunday by Sunday, the young John Wesley would have taken services in the small community, baptised their babies, celebrated their marriages and buried their dead. Some of the gravestones around the church commemorate the Wesleys' parishioners.

The parish church of St Pancras, Wroot

Wroot is also famous for Wroot Feast, held in the second week of July. People make floats to put in a competition and drive around the village in a parade. There are also competitions for scarecrows and fancy dress, which this year our school won. People put girls' names in a pot in the shop to vote for 'Miss Wroot'. This year, my friend Sophie from Wroot School was chosen. 'I rode in a float decorated with ribbons and glitter with two glamorous attendants. I felt very, very happy and special and I will be crowning the next Miss Wroot at the Wroot Feast.' We wondered how long Wroot Feast had been going for and whether there was one in the Wesleys' time here.
(by Louise R and Sophie R.)

While living at Wroot, John's sister, Hetty, the cleverest and most beautiful of all the Wesley girls met John Romley, John's predecessor as Curate. When Romley proposed marriage to Hetty, her father turned him down and sent Hetty away to work at Kelstern, near Louth. There she met a local lawyer, Will Atkins, and they fell in love. When Will asked the Rector if he could marry Hetty, Samuel refused him too as an *'unprincipled lawyer with a frivolous attitude to life'.* Hetty was bitterly disappointed and continued to see Will secretly until they decided to run away together to London.

After their first and only night together, she woke up to discover that he had changed his mind about marrying her. Abandoned in London, she had no choice but to return home to the Rectory. Heart-broken and worried that she might be pregnant, she promised her father to marry the first man who would have her. A local plumber agreed and Hetty began an appallingly unhappy married life. She tried to make peace with her parents by visiting them at Wroot with her first child, their grandchild, but they would not forgive her.

John Wesley did try to bring the family back together again but his efforts were hardly tactful. Preaching one Sunday in Wroot church, with his father and mother in the congregation, he chose as his theme *'Charity due to wicked persons'.* This just made Samuel angry with John and it took all of Charles' persuasive powers to reconcile father and son while Hetty remained unforgiven.

In the Wesleys' time, the curate at Wroot was also the schoolmaster at the Travis Charity school, which is still the Wroot primary school. A very poor boy called John Whitelamb was a pupil at the school and came into the Wesley story when he saved the Rector's life. *It was hard to get from Wroot to Epworth in wintertime because Wroot became an island. The path was flooded and you had to go on a boat to cross the rivers. The Rev Samuel Wesley had to preach at Epworth and John Whitelamb was rowing the boat to get him there. It was a stormy day when they set out*

and as they rowed, the sky got blacker and blacker. Eventually the rain came pouring down but they had to carry on. The storm got worse with waves banging on the sides of the boat and sending the boat flying about like a sweet wrapper in heavy wind. The boat got water-logged and began to sink. Samuel went overboard and started shouting because he couldn't swim. John Whitelamb grabbed him and swam him to the river bank. Samuel was so grateful, he said to John, 'you can come and stay with us'. So John went to live with the family at the Rectory.
(by Arran H and Rory G.)

Samuel Wesley was so impressed with John that he taught him Latin and Greek and encouraged him to go to Oxford University, where John Wesley was his tutor. Whitelamb returned to Wroot as Samuel's curate. *He again lived with the Wesleys for a time and fell in love with Samuel's daughter, Mary who was known as Molly. Molly had had an accident when she was a baby when someone dropped her. She was deformed but John did not mind. They got married at Wroot Church and lived happily together for a year. When Molly had a baby, the baby died and Molly died too. John was very upset but he carried on living in Wroot for thirty five more years till he died in 1769 aged sixty two.* *(by Frances T. and Gemma P.)*

> In Memory of John Whitelambe Rector Of this Parish 35 Years. Buried the 29th day of July 1769 Aged 62 Years Worthy of Imitation, thus at the cost Francis Wood Esq 1772

The Whitelamb memorial stone in Wroot church-yard by Gemma P.

> REMEMBER
> JOHN WESLEY
> founder of Methodism who served as curate in the Parish of Wroot during the years 1727-1729. When his father Samuel Wesley was the rector of Epworth.
> LORD LET ME NOT LIVE TO BE USELESS

The stone commemorating John Wesley's service in Wroot, by Holly J and Melissa B.

John Wesley later wrote about his early years of preaching: in Oxford, Epworth and Wroot: *'From the year 1725 to 1729 I preached much, but saw no fruit of my labour. Indeed, it could not be that I should; for I neither laid the foundation of repentance, nor of believing the Gospel; taking it for granted that all to whom I preached were believers, and that many of them needed no repentance.'*

The year after Molly died, Samuel Wesley fell ill. He died with John and Charles at his bedside and was buried in Epworth church-yard. John tried unsucessfully to take over as Rector of the parish but it was too late. Samuel Hurst had been appointed to the living with John Romley as his curate. This meant that Susanna and her remaining family had to move out of the Old Rectory and leave Epworth which had been their home for nearly forty years.

Barn Owl

Dragonfly

Bittern   Mute swan

Frog   Pike

The birds and beasts of Axholme by Arran H., Niall C., Louise R., Robert H., Samantha C. and Robyn W.

5. Going to America

Just before his father died, John Wesley decided that his lack of success in preaching in England might change if he tried preaching somewhere else. Colonies had been established all down the east coast of America, from New England to the Carolinas, but there was one area just north of the Spanish colony in Florida which had no European settlement. It was the home of the Creek Indians but an English General, James Oglethorpe, had been given a lease on the land to establish a colony, to be called Georgia in honour of the King. Samuel Wesley had written to Oglethorpe and given him a communion set to take to Georgia, offering also to go himself as a missionary, although he was an old man.

Memorial to the Wesleys' arrival in Georgia on Cockspur Island in February 1736 by Duncan M.

John was still a Fellow of Lincoln College but he decided to go to Georgia to *'preach to the Indians'* as a member of the Society for the Propagation of the Gospel, a plan which Susanna supported whole-heartedly. Although Charles was not yet ordained, John persuaded him to be ordained and prepare to come to Georgia with him. John Wesley was appointed as Chaplain to the Colony and Charles as Secretary to Governor Oglethorpe. With two Oxford friends, they set sail for Georgia with Oglethorpe, arriving in the new colony in February 1736.

Georgia Colony had been settled by the English in 1733 to prevent the Spanish from spreading any further north from Florida but it was also to be a new home for debtors from England's notorious prisons. At a time when most of those convicted of theft, let alone murder, were executed by hanging, those who fell into debt were held in prison until they could pay. Since they could not work to pay off their debt, many died in prison of hunger or disease. To transport some of them to America seemed more charitable.

18th century engraving showing early Savannah on the Yamacraw Bluff, as it was when the Wesleys reached Georgia.

The main settlement was at Savannah, then little more than a village of timber huts, although Oglethorpe had already planned a city with squares and wide streets in the forest clearing on the Yamacraw Bluff above the river. John took up his duties in the hut which served as a parsonage on what is now Reynolds Square, holding services for the settlers in the open air but they soon reacted badly to his strict church discipline and High Church practice.

While John was upsetting the families of Savannah, Charles travelled on with Oglethorpe in an open boat through the channel behind the sea-islands to a new settlement eighty miles to the south. They landed on St Simon's Island and established a base at Fort Frederica, where conditions were much more primitive than in Savannah.

Fort Frederica where Charles Wesley began his work in Georgia.

It is hardly surprising that Charles was soon in trouble. He had been a reluctant recruit to the venture, had accepted ordination in haste and was ill-prepared either for ministry or the rough life of the fort. He must have seemed an attractive target for abuse from the tough women of the London back-streets who were amongst his parishioners. Two of them soon made trouble by telling Charles lies about the Governor's behaviour towards them and then telling the Governor further lies about how Charles had behaved! Oglethorpe refused to speak to Charles and ordered the settlers to have nothing to do with him. With no house or equipment of his own, Charles was forced to sleep on the ground with very little to eat. He soon became very ill. John hurried down from Savannah and managed to persuade Oglethorpe that he had misjudged Charles, but Charles was too sick to go on. John agreed to take over his duties at Fort Frederica and Charles, disillusioned and discouraged as well as very sick, sailed for home.

John did not last much longer than Charles in Fort Frederica. He also found the conditions too rough and soon returned to Savannah to begin again, although he made four further short visits to St Simon's Island. While John and Charles were in Georgia, they met the Indian Chief Tomochichi and planned to preach to his Creek people. Charles is even shown in this 19th Century print apparently preaching to the Creek.

As the Creek spoke their own language, they would have thought that Wesley was speaking gibberish, so they seem to be sitting around doing their own thing. Charles read loads from the Bible and preached for ages but nobody seemed to listen.

(by Samantha C. and Rory G.)

Charles Wesley preaching to the Creek Indians

    Careful reading of the Wesleys' journals reveals that neither of them actually had a preaching ministry to any significant number of Creeks or any other Indian tribe. John's ministry was to the settlers of the young colony at both Savannah and Fort Frederica.

John Wesley as the 'sharp-nosed little parson' whom the people of Savannah came to dislike so much by Brett C.

But as so often with John, it was his relationship with a young woman that brought about his downfall. Sophy Hopkey was eighteen and the niece of a man who had been sent to the colony for fraud but then rose to become the chief magistrate! Sophy did all that she could to attract John's attention, visiting him, wearing clothes she knew he liked, nursing him when he fell ill and arranging for him to become her tutor. John gave every indication of falling in love with her but, as usual, could not actually bring himself to ask her to marry him. Her uncle decided that John would never make up his mind and encouraged his niece to marry another man.

John was furious and accused her of deliberately misleading him. He even decided to punish her by refusing to allow her to take communion, turning a private dispute into a very public affair. Sophy's uncle was furious and brought every charge he could against John, from meddling in family matters to altering the liturgy, using unauthorized hymns and baptising infants by triple immersion.

John Wesley's statue in Reynolds Square, Savannah, Georgia

Wesley was to be tried by a jury packed with friends of Sophy's family but the trial was repeatedly delayed. Taking his chance, he ran away as fast as he could, first to the Carolinas and then escaping on a ship sailing for England on Christmas Eve 1737. In every way, it seemed, the Wesley brothers had been abject failures in Georgia, but they had one experience there which would prove to be a turning point in both of their lives.

On the ship going out and when they returned to London, they met Moravian Christians who had escaped from persecution in Germany to seek a new life in America. John and Charles were deeply impressed by these men. They seemed sure of their faith and committed to a simple way of life, living in love and peace as the first Christians had done. Even when a violent storm struck their ship on the way to America, these Moravians were not afraid. It was as if they were calmly ready to meet God and sang hymns even at the height of the storm. When they reached Savannah, the Wesleys met other Moravians who also seemed certain of their faith and whose questions they found hard to answer.

Peter Bohler, the German Moravian, who so impressed the Wesleys

When John Wesley got back to London and linked up again with Charles, they met Peter Bohler, another Moravian. Bohler was a gifted speaker and an ordained minister. He was on his way from Germany to America where he planned to work as a missionary for the Moravian Church, amongst the African slaves who had been brought to work in the plantations of the Carolinas. In long talks with Bohler, both of the Wesleys were impressed by his deep sense of Christian peace. He encouraged them to think more of what God had done for them, rather than continuing to strive to do things for God.

6. Hearts strangely warmed

Charles and John invited Bohler to visit Oxford with them. While they were there, Charles fell ill again and was sure that he was going to die. At his bedside and taking him by the hand, Bohler prayed for his recovery and assured Charles, *'you will not die now'*. Later, Bohler met up with John Wesley who had to admit that he had not experienced Christian joy, peace and love in his life, but remained fearful, had doubts and continued to sin. According to the Moravians, this meant that he was not a true Christian. How then could he continue as a preacher? Bohler offered him the advice: *'Preach faith until you have it and then, because you have it, you will preach faith.'*

When Bohler left them to continue on his journey to America, Charles was still very ill with pleurisy. He was carried to the house of an uneducated man called John Bray. There he read Martin Luther's Commentary on the Letter to the Galatians, in which Luther discovers for himself that faith was the gift of God, not the reward for trying to please God with good works. Charles was still very ill when John

Bray read to him the verse in Matthew 9 in which Jesus says to the paralysed man: *'Son, be of good cheer, thy sins are forgiven thee.'* Charles heard these words as a direct message from God and on the following day, Whitsunday 1738, he was overwhelmed with a sense of God's forgiveness. *'I now found myself at peace with God, and rejoiced in hope of loving Christ.'*

Three days later in the very early morning, John Wesley was reading the 2nd Letter of Peter including the words *'thou art not far from the kingdom of God'*. Later that day, he went to Choral Evensong at St Paul's Cathedral, where the anthem for the day was, *'Out of the deep have I called unto thee, O Lord; Lord, hear my voice....'* Then in the evening, John went, according to his journal entry *'very unwillingly to a society in Aldersgate Street where one was reading Luther's Preface to the Epistle to the Romans. About a quarter before nine, while he was describing the change which God works in the heart through faith in Christ, I felt my heart strangely warmed. I felt I did trust in Christ, Christ alone for salvation; and an assurance was given me that he had taken away my sins, even mine, and saved me from the law of sin and death.'*

Within a few days, both John and Charles Wesley had been changed from self-critical failures to self-confident followers of the God whose love now flowed through them to the people around them. Their huge talents, John as a preacher and organiser and Charles as the writer of hymns, were released to be used by God to grow His Church right across England and beyond England to the world. But it did not all happen at once and the first reaction to their new-found faith was very negative. John Wesley's friends were suspicious of his sudden change of heart and churches in London banned him from their pulpits because what he now taught – complete and instant conversion – offended against their doctrines.

He decided to travel to Germany and on the way visited Susanna, his mother, who was staying in Salisbury. She too thought his new views *'extravagent and enthusiastic'* and when he asked for her blessing, she refused him. John nevertheless went on to visit the Moravian settlements and to meet their founder, Count Zinzendorf. Although the Moravians refused to allow him to take communion with them and encouraged him to work humbly in their garden, John regarded them as *'living witnesses to the reality of saving by faith.'* When he returned to England, he wrote enthusiastically about his experience to both his older brother, Samuel, and his sister, Emily. She had looked after their mother when their father died and was struggling with a disastrous marriage and real poverty.

Samuel had become the very respectable and successful Headmaster of Blundell's School in Tiverton. As the head of the family he wrote back to John reminding him that he was still a Church of England priest, and rebuking him for seeming to abandon the authodox Anglican views which he should be promoting. Emily's reply was more bitter. *'Dear brother, Yours I received, and thank you for remembering me, though your letter afforded me little consolation. For God's sake, tell me how a distressed woman, who expects daily to have the very bed taken from under her for rent, can consider the state of the churches in Germany.'*

Throughout this time, John continued to receive money as a Fellow of Lincoln College, Oxford, although he gave up any pretence of fulfilling his duties there. He now knew the difference that God's love could make in his life and he wanted to link up with others who had shared this experience. One of the members of the 'Oxford Holy Club', George Whitefield, had followed the Wesleys to Georgia. Before he left England, Whitefield had an experience which transformed his life: *'O! with what joy – joy unspeakable was my soul filled, when the weight of sin fell off, and an abiding sense of the pardoning love of God, and an assurance of faith broke in upon my disconsolate soul!'*

When he got to Georgia, Whitefield gained the respect of the colonists by helping them in practical ways and captivating them by his powerful preaching and charismatic personality. His time in the colony was as successful as the Wesleys' had been traumatic. Whitefield returned to England to meet up again with John and Charles and to raise funds for an orphanage project which had first been proposed by Charles. He travelled to Bristol, preaching and fund-raising en-route and met up with Susanna Wesley. She was very impressed both with Whitefield's sincerity and his good reports of what John and Charles were trying to do.

But when Whitefield was refused permission to preach in the Bristol churches because of his '*enthusiasm*', he turned to preaching in the open air, as he and the Wesleys had done in Georgia. He knew that others had already done this especially in Wales where Howell Harris had preached to crowds of miners even though he was not ordained. Soon Whitefield was holding open-air meetings in the Bristol area and preaching to crowds of thousands many times each week. Having promised to return to Georgia, Whitefield wrote to John Wesley to ask him to come to Bristol to take advantage of the *'glorious door opened amongst the colliers. You must come and water what God has enabled me to plant.'*

John agreed and joined Whitefield when he preached to the miners of Kingswood, just outside Bristol. He saw how moved the men were by Whitefield's preaching and reluctantly decided that he too should preach in the open air. Whitefield also gave him money for a school for the children of the Kingswood miners and left Bristol to prepare for his return to Georgia from London. John Wesley took over his preaching in the Bristol area giving five hundred sermons in the first nine months of his time there. Only eight of these were in churches. The crowds that came to hear him were smaller than those who were attracted by Whitefield but John Wesley had become a committed *'field-preacher'*. He compared his role to that of Christ in the Sermon on the Mount, and saying *'I now have no parish of my own, nor probably ever shall....I look upon all the world as my parish…this is the work I know God has called me to, and I am sure that His blessing attends it.'*

Back in London, Whitefield met up with Charles and tried to persuade him to become a field-preacher as well, but Charles refused to upset the church by holding such meetings. Whitefield preached to thousands in Moorfields and on Kennington Common with Charles at his side and Howell Harris added his persuasive powers but Charles still resisted. When he preached to a small congregation at a village church in Essex, he was asked by a local farmer to preach again outside, in a field. When five hundred came to hear him, Charles was torn between his obedience to the Church and his wish to reach as many people as possible. In the town of Thaxted, the question was resolved for him. When he was refused permission to preach in the church, he was invited to preach in the neighbouring field to seven hundred and on the following day to one thousand listeners.

Charles was convinced that this was what God wanted him to do, but the Church in the person of the Archbishop of Canterbury was determined to stop him. Threatened with excommunication and dismissal as an Anglican Priest for his unauthorised preaching, it seemed to Charles that the Church was driving him towards the very activity that they so objected to. Whitefield then pre-empted his decision by announcing that Charles would preach in Moorfields on the 24th June. When Charles got there, he found *'near ten thousand helpless sinners waiting for the word... The Lord was with me, even me, his meanest messenger, according to his promise.. my load was gone, and all my doubts and scruples. God shone upon my path, and I knew THIS was his will concerning me.'*

The New Room, Bristol by Rory G.

With Charles and Whitefield in London, John continued to preach in Bristol. He decided that his followers needed two 'preaching houses' in the city to protect those who came to hear his sermons from hostile crowds. One was built in Bristol at the Horsefair and became the 'New Room', the first Methodist Chapel to be built anywhere in the world. It is still a centre for Methodist worship in the city. The second development started as a school, for both boys and girls, and as a preaching house. But a rival school was set up a mile away and John Wesley later decided to set up yet another, as a boarding school for the sons of his preachers. This grew into Kingswood School, which later moved to Bath. The original buildings of both the miners' school and Kingswood School were demolished by 1917. Only the pulpit from the preaching house survives in the hall of the current Kingswood School.

When George Whitefield returned to America, John Wesley continued with the work in London. Charles took over in Bristol although constant preaching and the strain of opposition made him ill. In both major centres the Wesleys set up 'societies' divided into bands or 'classes', small groups of about a dozen regular worshippers who met together much as the original 'Holy Club' had done. Each society also committed themselves to giving to the poor and for the provision of a building to meet in, while still retaining their membership of the Church of England. The Wesleys insisted that these societies should only meet at times which did not clash with the services of the local parish church, so that they could not be accused of setting up a rival church.

In London, John Wesley was offered a large and derelict building in Windmill Street to hire and convert into a preaching house. It had once been used as a royal gun foundry, but an explosion and years of neglect had reduced it to a ruin. It was both cheap and in a strategic place near to the City. John had no money, but was lent the funds to lease and repair it while he organised societies to use the building and to raise the money. He started to preach in the midst of the ruins even before the work was finished and the Foundry became the London headquarters of a society which rapidly grew to over three hundred members.

The Foundry, John Wesley's London base for over thirty years, until the City Road Chapel was opened in 1778.

With bases established in London and Bristol, John Wesley next rode north, through Yorkshire to Newcastle-upon-Tyne. He knew no-one in the city but with one companion, John Taylor, stood in one of the poorer streets and began to sing. *'Praise God from whom all blessings flow........'*, the familiar words of the Doxology. A small crowd gathered and soon grew to several hundred. Wesley preached to them, and again in the evening to even more. The people of Tyneside were ready to hear the gospel he preached and many were moved to respond.

He found a site for a meeting house in Newcastle on land off what is now Northumberland Street and the 'Orphan House' was built, the name referring to Whitefield's plan to build an orphanage in Georgia. It was the largest Methodist meeting house in the country and soon the first Sunday School was established there. Wesley needed someone to oversee the activities at the Orphan House and, in 1845, he chose a remarkable young widow who had been active at the Foundry before returning to her native Tyneside. Her name was Grace Murray and she not only managed the property, including looking after visiting preachers, but was also a preacher herself.

7. Riding through England

With three bases in London, Bristol and Newcastle established, both John and Charles Wesley could visit the scattered societies of Methodists in the towns and villages of England and continue their preaching to any who would listen. They both rode back and forth across the country, with occasional visits to Cornwall, Wales, Scotland and over the sea to Ireland. Wherever they went, they preached to the people, in the few churches which would still allow them entry or in the squares and fields where they were not.

John Wesley and his horse travelled about a quarter of a million miles together very happily along the roads of England. That's about the same as ten time round the Earth at the Equator or the distance from the Earth to the Moon! When John got on the horse, he let the reins go loose. The horse trotted along as good as gold while John read his bible, not looking where they were going. Every so often, the horse fell into a hole or a ditch, but John just got back on, and the horse would trot on again.

(by Gemma P. and Edward F.)

John Wesley on his horse by Alex A.

Many of his journeys to and from the north of England included a visit to Epworth as it lay roughly at the centre of the 'Methodist triangle' of the three major cities. On his way back from his first visit to Newcastle, travelling with John Taylor, they called in at Epworth. Wesley had not been back to the town since his father's death, seven years before and he was not sure how well he would be received. He stayed overnight at the Red Lion Inn in the Market Square, and found that they remembered him with affection.

Next morning he attended the service at the Parish Church and asked the Curate if he would like him to pray or to preach. Mr Romley, the man who had quarrelled with the Wesleys over his courting of Hetty, would not allow him back into the pulpit. So John Taylor stood at the door of the church and told the people after the service to come back in the evening.

When he was not allowed to preach in the church, John Wesley stood on his dad's grave and preached to a crowd of people in the church-yard. *(by Louis L.)*

In his journal he wrote: *'I am well assured that I did far more good to them by preaching three days from my father's tomb than I did by preaching three years in his pulpit.'*

Samuel Wesley's tomb in Epworth Church-yard by Victoria J.

On another occasion while visiting Epworth and staying at the Red Lion, John Wesley left a lasting impression on one young listener.

'I was working in the Red Lion Inn, when this short, smart looking man come in. I thought I recognised him and offered him a pint of beer on the house. "I do not drink alcohol thank you very much," he said. Next day, John Wesley went out to the Market Place to stand on the steps of the Market Cross and preach to a crowd of the people of Epworth who had gathered there. Some of the people did not like him but he just got on with it and many listened to him. He came back to Epworth many times but I will never forget that day I heard him preach.'

(by Ross B.)

The Red Lion Inn in Epworth by Albert C.

To get to and from Epworth to other parts of the country at that time, travellers had to cross the River Trent by ferry as there were no bridges. About three miles south-east of the town, the village of Owston Ferry grew up around the crossing point. Especially in bad weather and when the tidal bore or Aegre ran up the Trent, the crossing could be hazardous. Travellers would have to wait at the inns in the village until the ferrymen agreed to take them over. One evening in 1742, John Wesley and his followers were waiting at Owston to cross the Trent, when a crowd gathered.

'As I pushed my way through the huge, noisy crowd on the bank of the river Trent in our village, a man climbed onto the mounting block outside the White Hart. He stood high above the heads of the crowd with a joyful yet serious looking face and long hair. He began to speak with a deep low voice and preached to us all with love until late into the evening. I walked away feeling strange yet different. Then I realised I was a changed man.'

(by Rosie P.)

By late evening, the weather was breaking, with a rising wind and threat of rain. The boatmen were very reluctant to set out, but Wesley and his friends persuaded them to risk the crossing, taking their horses with them in the boat.

Crossing the Trent

Silver storm clouds gathered way up high,
Lightning flashes in the midnight sky,
Heavy raindrops fall and thunder gives a mighty rumble,
The boat begins to rock - the passengers tumble,
In a sudden bolt our horses are overboard,
I pray "Have mercy on us, Lord!"
A vigorous shake of the boat and a crash of waves...
This dangerous trip could send us all to watery graves.
Suddenly, my foot gets caught......
For one long moment, I was completely distraught.
Then we reach the bank, thanks to the skill of our men,
And the ferryboat sets off back again.
We eventually arrived in Grimsby – everyone still safe,
Mainly because of God's everlasting grace.

(By Ellie G and Leigh N-A)

On his travels, Wesley faced many other hazards. In some places the crowds proved hostile and did their best to disrupt his meetings. Even the Magistrates tried to stop him preaching, claiming that he was disturbing the peace. John Wesley continued undeterred and at the height of the opposition travelled to Wednesbury, north-west of Birmingham, where the houses of Methodists had been attacked by a rioting mob.

John Wesley facing the mob in Wednesbury

'A man arrived at the Wednesbury Inn yesterday. He was small in stature, serious looking and seemed extremely snobby. He sat down to eat and began to read a book - it was the Bible. After reading right through his dinner, he left to go to bed upstairs without saying much to me or anyone else.

In the morning, I saw a crowd of people gathered outside the inn. As it was my break, I went to see what was going on. The people looked fierce and angry and then I realised why. The strange looking man was preaching about God and Jesus. Everybody was so annoyed. I was quite irritated myself but he was really calm and just kept speaking and reading out loud from his Bible. Some people started to throw things at him and threaten him with knives and axes but he stayed extremely calm until he had finished what he wanted to say. I never saw that man again but I cannot forget that day.' *(by Finn K.)*

Towards the end of his life, John wrote *'I rode to Epworth, which I still love beyond most places in the world'*.

8. Singing the gospel

While John Wesley was preaching and organising his new societies, Charles was also busy, writing hymns, thousands of hymns. His was a unique talent – taking the experience and ideas of the early Methodists and turning them into verse which could be set to music and sung to the glory of God. Most churches of the time did not use hymns in worship, preferring to follow the Prayer Book and chanting the Psalm set for the day. There was a growing interest in having musicians to accompany the singing and Charles Wesley's hymns brought music into the heart of worship.

His father, Samuel, had written hymns and while at Westminster School, Charles would have been immersed in Church music of the highest quality. On the day in which Charles found forgiveness for himself, he also found a verse from the Bible (Ps 40 v 3.): '*He hath put a new song in my mouth, even a thanksgiving unto our God,*' which he believed applied to him. Two days later he wrote a 'new song'

> *Where shall my wondering soul begin?*
> *How shall I all to heaven aspire?*
> *A slave redeemed from death and sin,*
> *A brand plucked from eternal fire,*
> *How shall I equal triumphs raise,*
> *Or sing my great deliverer's praise?*

When John had his own overwhelming experience of forgiveness two days after that, Charles and John could join together to sing *'their great deliverer's praise'* in the words of the new hymn. From then onwards, for fifty years, hymns poured out of Charles Wesley as fast as sermons poured out of his brother.

Charles wrote the well known Christmas carol:

> *Hark! The herald angels sing,*
> *Glory to the new-born King,*
> *Peace on earth, and mercy mild,*
> *God and sinners reconciled.*
> *Joyful, all ye nations rise,*
> *Join the triumph of the skies;*
> *With the angelic host proclaim:*
> *'Christ is born in Bethlehem.'*
>   *Hark! The herald angels sing*
>   *Glory to the newborn king.*

and a hymn to celebrate Easter:

> *Christ the Lord is risen today;*
>   *Alleluia!*
> *Sons of men and angels say:*
> *Raise your joys and triumphs high;*
> *Sing ye heavens; thou earth reply*
>   *Alleluia!*

One of his hymns is still very popular for weddings:

> *Love divine, all loves excelling,*
>   *Joy of heaven to earth come down,*
> *Fix in us thy humble dwelling,*
>   *All thy faithful mercies crown.*
> *Jesu, thou art all compassion,*
>   *Pure, unbounded love thou art;*
> *Visit us with thy salvation,*
>   *Enter every trembling heart.*

And another of his hymns is voted into the top ten hymns each year:

> *O for a thousand tongues to sing*
> *My great Redeemer's praise*
> *The glories of my God and King,*
> *The triumphs of his grace!*

For a time, Charles returned to his ministry to the most despised members of society, prostitutes held in the Marshalsea and condemned prisoners held in Newgate Prison. Having spoken to them in their cells, he travelled with the condemned in the cart on the way to the gallows at Tyburn and was there at their hanging. *'We left them going to meet their Lord........When the cart drew off, not one stirred, or struggled for life, but meekly gave up their spirits..... That hour under the gallows was the most blessed hour of my life.'*

Charles joined John in travelling throughout England and pioneered the work in Cornwall. He faced the same dangers from mobs and was pelted by stones, eggs and dirt in Yorkshire. He went to Wednesbury and faced the same men who had threatened John. To encourage Methodists facing persecution, Charles put together a collection of his hymns which he called *'Hymns for Time of Trouble'*. Opposition to the Methodists grew as they were suspected of being Jacobites, plotting to replace George II with Bonnie Prince Charlie. Although there was no truth in this allegation, it was a dangerous time to be seen to be holding what appeared to be secret gatherings.

With England now covered by a network of Methodist societies, the Wesleys next turned to Ireland. John decided that Charles should go to Dublin to support the small group of Methodists who had started a work there and Charles set out via Wales. On his journey, he stayed with a Methodist family who had a very pretty daughter, Sarah

Gwynne, known as Sally. Charles was twice her age but captivated by her beauty. *'At first sight my soul seemed pleased to take acquaintance with thee. And never have I found such a nearness to any creature as to you.'*

Charles journeyed on to Ireland and found in Dublin a violence against the Methodists which made the English mobs seems relatively tame. Undaunted, he encouraged the small groups of Methodists to set up meeting places where they could at least get some shelter and travelled across Ireland facing violent opposition wherever he went.

9. Marriages made in heaven ?

Charles Wesley came back from his visit to Ireland exhausted and ill. He reached the Gwynne's home in Wales after riding for days through appalling weather and was put to bed for a fortnight. Nursed back to health by Sally, he was sure that she was the one for him but he was afraid of what John would say when he told him of his love for her. They had earlier agreed to consult each other before getting married. There was another problem in that Charles was in no position to support a wife, with no income, a fact which troubled Sally's parents.

In the end, John did agree and solved the other problem as well. He had published collections of Charles' hymns which had sold well. Out of the income, John Wesley promised to give Charles an allowance of £100 a year – enough to support them both. Sally and Charles were married in a little church in Wales in 1749 and began their very happy married life together. For a time, Charles continued to travel around England, preaching and supporting his brother, but he found that family life at 4, Charles Street, Bristol, led him to give up this wandering and settle down. He and Sally had three children who survived infancy and both of their sons were talented musicians. When they moved to London, Charles arranged for the boys to give concerts at home to leading members of London society.

Shortly after Charles' marriage he heard that John was himself planning to marry. Grace Murray, the housekeeper at the Newcastle Orphan House, had nursed John back to health while he had been ill in Newcastle, and he had told her *'if ever I marry I think you will be the person.'* Grace travelled with him as he preached through the North of England, and he then left her in Lancashire in the company of another preacher, John Bennett. Bennett had also been nursed by Grace and he too had decided that God was calling him to marry her. John Wesley certainly knew of the relationship between Grace and Bennett but still chose to take Grace with him on his next visit to Ireland. In Dublin they signed a civil agreement which amounted to a marriage and when they got back to England, John decided to meet with both Grace and Bennett at Epworth. They tried to resolve the confusion but who should marry whom was still unclear, to Grace, to Bennett and to John Wesley. He could not make up his mind, just as he had failed to do with Sally Kirkham and Sophy Hopkey.

Matters became even more complicated when Charles heard of the proposed marriage with Grace. He rushed north to try to stop his brother becoming inextricably linked to a woman who seemed to Charles to have dishonestly accepted two offers of marriage. She was also of a much lower social class than John and perhaps this was what Charles really objected to. In the end, Charles persuaded Grace to ride with him to Newcastle where Charles conducted a wedding between John Bennett and Grace Murray, bringing the whole muddled tale to an end.

Not long afterwards, Charles Wesley met a wealthy widow, Mary Vazeille, and through him, she met John. He had finally decided that he was much in need of a wife who would shield him from other women. Mary was far too old to have children and so would not distract John from his travelling and preaching by giving him family responsibilities.

John also thought that she had other merits. *'I admire your indefatigable industry,'* he wrote to her, *'your exact frugality, your uncommon neatness and the cleanness both of your person, your clothes and all things around you.'* His letter to Mary was hardly romantic, but he had at last decided to marry. In February 1751, John Wesley and Mary Vazeille were married in London, but it soon proved to be a disastrous match.

She accused him of marrying her for her money although he settled most of it on her and her son from a previous marriage shortly after the wedding. She refused to accompany him on his preaching journeys, which was probably just as well as she could cause trouble wherever she went. She searched his pockets, read his letters, lost her temper, and even assaulted him, tearing out his hair. She hated Charles and accused his wife, Sally, of being John's mistress. She threatened to leave him, which she did, much to his relief. He wrote to her listing his dislikes from *'1. sharing any one of my letters, 2. being made a prisoner in my own house, 3. talking about me behind my back etc'* up to 10, followed by ten pieces of advice, each telling her to stop one of the dislikes. She did reappear, briefly, but it must have been a relief to him to hear, in 1781, that she had died.

Only Charles out of Susanna Wesley's ten children had a truly long and happy marriage. Samuel's was cut short by his relatively early death at 49. All of the girls had love affairs, and their father at first interpreted the strange noises in the Rectory to the girls sitting up late or to their lovers' visits, rather than to a ghost. But the Rector disapproved of most of the men who came to court the girls, and Susanna played her part in rejecting some. The seven faced most of the frustrations, anxieties, financial disasters and domestic violence which keep the best soap operas going today.

They all inherited Susanna's beauty and determination. Emily, the eldest stayed at Epworth until she was 33 and then moved to London. She met a friend of her brother's, Robert Leybourne, and was swept off her feet. But she could not find work in London and Robert could not marry as he was dependant on an Oxford fellowship only open to single men. She had to return to Epworth, where Susanna's strong disapproval and Emily's obedience to her mother's command, destroyed their relationship. When she was in her forties, she did get married to a man who made use of what little money she had and died after five years. As a widow, Emily became sharp-tongued and bitter, although she eventually mellowed and served the needy at a Methodist Chapel in London.

Sukey made, on the face of it, a successful marriage with her father's approval although her mother's misgivings proved to be a better assessment. Richard Ellison was, as has been said, wealthy and together they rented the Epworth Rectory when the Wesleys decided to live at the Wroot parsonage. But by 1730, as Ellison's wealth dwindled so his violent behaviour towards Sukey grew until she left him, moving to London with their four children to live with her sister Anne.

Mary's short and tragic story at Wroot and that of her sister Hetty's marriage to a drunken and wife-beating plumber have already been told. Hetty did eventually find forgiveness from her mother but was never reconciled to her father. Her health failed and she too died relatively young at 53.

Anne was born one of twins but her brother died in infancy. She grew up in the Rectory and then worked for a time as a governess. She married a local surveyor, John Lambert, and with him had a son. By all accounts they were a happy family and John Wesley was godfather to their son. They moved to London where John took to drinking heavily, often with Hetty's husband. Anne cared for John Wesley when he became ill at the Foundry but when she died or where she was buried remain a mystery.

The two youngest girls, Martha and Kezia, were very different characters but linked romantically to the same man. Martha was intelligent and quick to learn. John taught her to write in Susanna's Rectory 'school' but she had little sense of humour. She went to stay with her uncle in London as a teenager, and when she returned to the family, she had a succession of suitors, including her father's curate, John Romley at Wroot. She also met all the young men from Oxford who came to visit the family through John's and Charles' involvement in the Holy Club. Westley Hall was one of them and he and Martha fell in love. Without the consent of either Samuel or Susanna, he proposed and she agreed to marry him as soon as they could,

When Westley Hall next visited Epworth, he met her sister, Kezia or Kezzy as the family called her. Westley claimed that God was now telling him to marry Kezzy, giving her a friendship ring to be replaced as soon as possible by a wedding ring. When he returned to London and met Martha again, he, and apparently God, changed his mind yet again and he decided he would marry Martha. There was a furious row in the family with poor Kezzy accused of trying to steal Westley from Martha but Martha did become Mrs Westley Hall. They had ten children, only one of whom survived infancy.

After a time of happiness together, Westley began to see other women and had a number of illegitimate children before leaving Martha to go to seek his fortune in the West Indies. Martha lived in London and got to know Dr Samuel Johnson, visiting him to discuss the books and plays she so enjoyed reading. She was the last of the Wesley children to die, just after John's death in 1791, and she was buried with him in the vault behind Wesley's Chapel in London.

10. Practical help for the poor

Even while they were still at Oxford, both John and Charles Wesley believed that they should do all that they could for the poor and disadvantaged. John found that he could live on £28 per year, if he avoided spending money on things he regarded as unnecesary such as hair-cuts and wearing a wig. What he saved, he gave to the poor. He put into practice his teaching: *'Do all the good you can, by all the means you can, in all the ways you can, in all the places you can, at all the times you can, to all the people you can, as long as ever you can.'*

He was particularly interested in scientific and medical experiments and was fascinated by the use of electricity. Persuading his followers that passing an electric shock through the body could have beneficial effects, he bought a machine which generated charge so that he and his friends could have what amounted to electric shock parties, with a serious purpose.

He wrote a book called Primitive Physic which means 'simple medicine', to help poor people when they were ill and didn't have enough money to get a doctor. Some plants and herbs are good for you but some are poisons, so the book helps you to know which are which. Our school helped to make the Physic Garden at the Old Rectory by planting the plants and herbs.

(by Rebecca M. and Sarah M.)

PRIMITIVE PHYSIC:

OR,

An EASY and NATURAL METHOD

OF

C U R I N G

MOST

D I S E A S E S.

By *JOHN WESLEY*, M.A.

Homo sum; humani nihil a me alienum puto.

THE TWENTY-FOURTH EDITION.

L O N D O N:

Printed by G. PARAMORE, *North-Green, Worship-Street;* And sold by G. WHITFIELD, at the Chapel, City-Road, and at all the Methodist Preaching-Houses in Town and Country. 1792.

The Physic Garden is a place of relaxation and reflection and has a collection of herbs, vegetables, soft fruit and fruit trees, many of the plants for the 'remedies' which Wesley included in his book. For example: *'To cure heartburning – chew fennel or parsley, and swallow your spittle – sometimes a vomit is needful!'*

11. The world-wide parish

Right up to their deaths, John and Charles Wesley remained ordained clergymen of the Church of England, although the development of the Methodist Societies across the United Kingdom and in the American Colonies caused increasing tensions between them. When the Americans under George Washington won their freedom by defeating the British at Yorktown, most of the clergy in the colonies came back to England, although Francis Asbury remained in America as leader of the Methodist Societies there. John Welsey tried to persuade the Bishop of London to ordain more clergy for America, but failed. He therefore decided to secretly ordain three men, one of whom, Thomas Coke, was already a priest. Coke was ordained as *'superintendent for America'* and the other two as *'presbyters for America'*.

Wesley justified this breach of Church law by claiming that in the early days of the church, there had been little distinction between priests and bishops and therefore he as a priest could perform some of the functions of a bishop, including ordination. Charles Wesley was horrified when he discovered what his brother had done and, true to character, composed a poem:

> *How easy now are bishops made*
> *At man or woman's whim.*
> *Wesley his hand on Coke hath laid,*
> *But who laid hands on him?*

Once Coke reached Maryland, he met with Asbury and ordained him as the first Bishop of the Methodist Church in America. The American Methodist Church now had a leadership independent of the Wesleys and could operate under its own 'conference'. The church flourished and grew to become the second largest Christian denomination in North America with a vigorous overseas missionary work which continues to this day. Charles Wesley foresaw the consequences of John's actions and the inevitable break with the Church of England. They were never reconciled over the issue of ordination, although both remained loyal to the Church until their deaths.

The ordination of Francis Asbury in Baltimore in 1787

Charles Wesley died in 1788 and was buried in the church-yard of Marylebone Parish Church, the church in which his parents were married. John lived on in his house next to the City Road Chapel, and although increasingly frail went on preaching in the open air and in Methodist chapels. He learned of the efforts of the movement to end the slave trade, a national scandal about which he had written in his

'Thoughts on Slavery' in 1774. In the final months of his life he wrote to William Wilberforce to encourage him to *'go on in the name of God and in the power of his might, till even American slavery (the vilest that ever saw the sun) shall banish before it.'*

John Wesley's death-bed scene, 2nd March 1791, from an old print

When John died in the tiny room in his house, all his friends were there. In this picture, he is shown sitting up because they thought that the only time you lay on your back was when you were in your coffin. One of his friends had an ear trumpet which helped him to hear John's last words 'The best of all is, God is with us'. All the people paid to be in the picture and had to give the artist pictures of themselves so that they could be recognised.
(by Ryan B. and Stephanie O.)

At about 10 am on 2nd March 1791, John tried to sing *'I'll praise my maker while I've breath'* but could manage no more than *'I'll praise.......'* before he died. He was 88. He left instructions for his funeral *'without undue ceremony'* and was buried as he had instructed, *'there shall be no hearse, no coach, no escutcheon, no pomp except the tears of those who love me and are following me to Abraham's bosom.'* He was carried to his grave by six poor men at five o'clock in the morning. His tomb is just behind the City Road Chapel, known as the 'mother-church of Methodism'.

12. The triumphs of his grace

This is the story of how God used a family, and in particular two of their sons, to bring about a triumph of his grace in spite of all their failures. Just as God used the flawed humanity of Jacob and David, Peter and Paul, to tell his people of his love for them and all humanity, so he used John and Charles Wesley in their day to bring new faith and new hope to the thousands who heard them. Theirs was, in many ways, a dysfunctional family but for all their faults, the Wesleys never lost their faith in a God of love and their commitment to sharing that faith with the world of their day.

Their story did not end in 1791. By that time, there were about 79,000 members of Methodist Societies in Britain and a similar number in the young United States of America. Since then, the Methodist Church has spread across the world so that today there are about 75 million Methodists world-wide, with the 8.5 million members of the American United Methodist Church forming the largest part of the church. The Methodist Churches in Korea, the Phillipines and in parts of Africa are among the fastest growing parts of the church today.

In towns and villages all over England, there are about 6000 active Methodist Churches with about 330,000 members. In some places, the signs of past divisions are still there, with 'Wesleyan', 'Primitive' or 'United' carved into brick and stone, but they have come together again in most communities to form one strong Methodist Church. Even the divisions between the Methodists and the Church of England are breaking down with the Covenant between the two churches committing both to work together wherever possible.

Methodists have gone all over the world to found new churches and the name of Epworth has gone with them. There are Epworths in Georgia and Iowa, in Zimbabwe and Australia. There is even an Epworth Scale to rival the Richter Scale for earthquakes, although this is a scale of Sleepiness, thanks to the research of the Epworth Hospital in Melbourne, Australia, and it has nothing to do with long sermons!

The Wesley Memorial Church in Epworth, England by Albert C.

Sources

We used the following books and published material to research this book:

Best, Gary *'Charles Wesley'* Epworth Press 2006

Ella, Colin *'The Isle of Axholme'* 2007

Greetham, Mary *'Susanna Wesley – Mother of Methodism'* Foundery Press 2003

Greetham, Mary and Peter *'Samuel Wesley'* Foundery Press 1990

Hattersley, Roy *'A Brand from the Burning'* Little, Brown 2002

Maser, Frederick E. *'The Wesley Sisters'* Foundery Press 1990

Newton, John A. *'Susanna Wesley and the Puritan Tradition in Methodism'* 2nd Ed. Epworth Press 2002

Pitkin Guides *'Wesley's Chapel'* 1994 Pitkin Unichrome

Vickers, John A. *'Charles Wesley'* Foundery Press 1990

Vickers, John A. *'John Wesley – Founder of Methodism'* Methodist Publishing House, 1977

Wakefield, Gordon S. *'John Wesley'* 2nd Ed. Foundery Press 2003

Thanks

We are very grateful to Mrs Joan Sidaway, the Curator, and her team of guides at the Old Rectory for help with this project and to the Trustees for permission to use pictures and photographs from the Old Rectory. Rev David Leese, Superintendent Minister of the Epworth Circuit has encouraged us and Mrs Paulette Bissell, Lincoln Diocese RE Advisor, suggested and supported the project. Rev David Hanson of Epworth by the Sea, Georgia provided information about the Wesleys in Georgia.

The project would not have been possible without the support of the Governors, Staff and Pupils of the four schools involved. Particular thanks to Mrs Sarah Groves, Headteacher, and Miss Sally Thomas, formerly Y6 Teacher, of Belton All Saints CE Primary School, to Miss Jo Pitchforth, Headteacher, and Mrs Alison Richardson, Y5/6 Teacher of St Martin's CE Primary School, Owston Ferry, to Mrs Chris Cook, Headteacher, and Mrs Mary Allen, KS2 Teacher, of Wroot Travis CE Primary School, and Mrs Pat Ward, former Headteacher, and Mr Christian Morris, Y5 Teacher, of Epworth Primary School.

The project was funded by a generous grant from the Trustees of the Westhill Endowment Fund for which we are very grateful.

The Rev Kathleen Richardson, Baroness Richardson of Callow, OBE, former President of Conference of the Methodist Church, very kindly agreed to launch our book in Epworth on 9th February 2009.

John Haden
2009